THE
BIG
BOOK
OF
BUGS

Words and pictures
YUVAL ZOMMER

Bug expert
BARBARA TAYLOR

Can you find ...
... exactly the same fly 15 times in
this book? Watch out for imposters.

THE BIG BOOK OF BUGS

Thames & Hudson

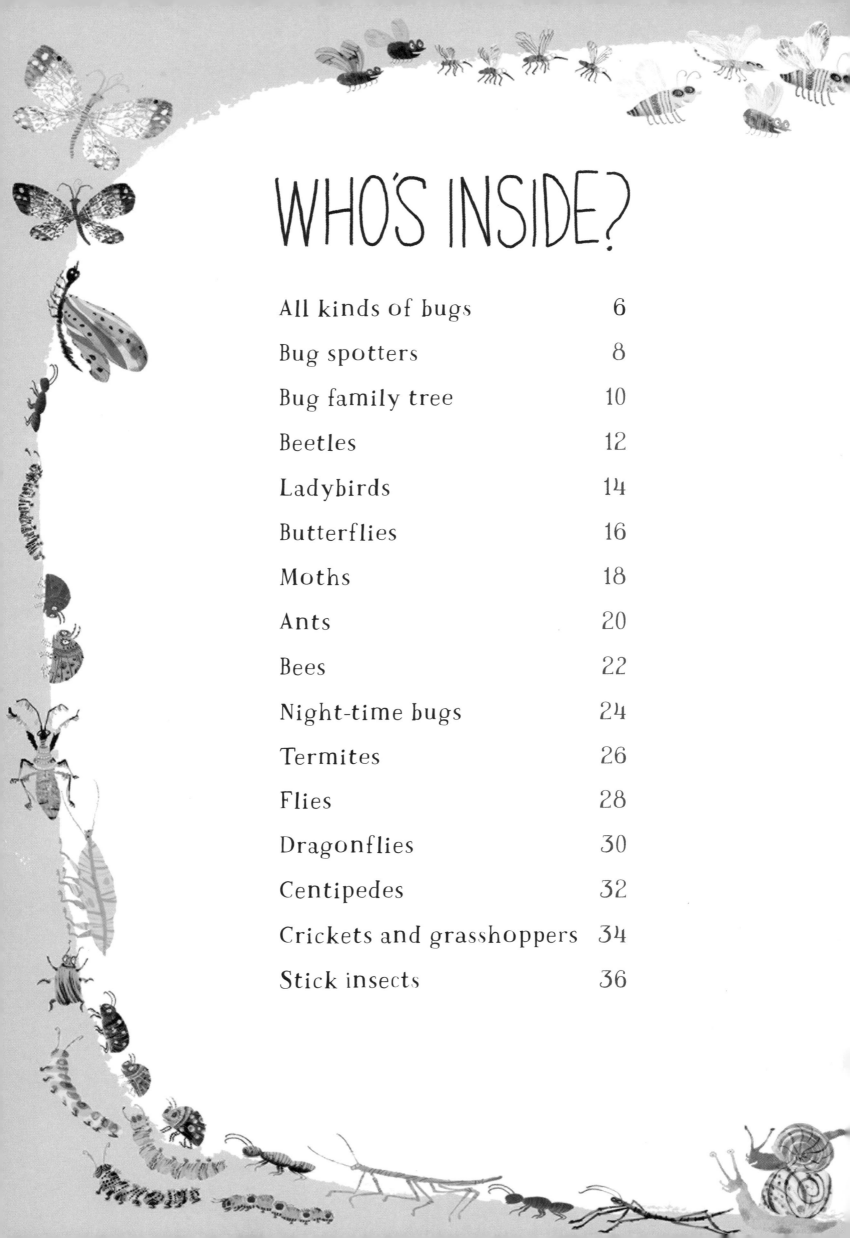

WHO'S INSIDE?

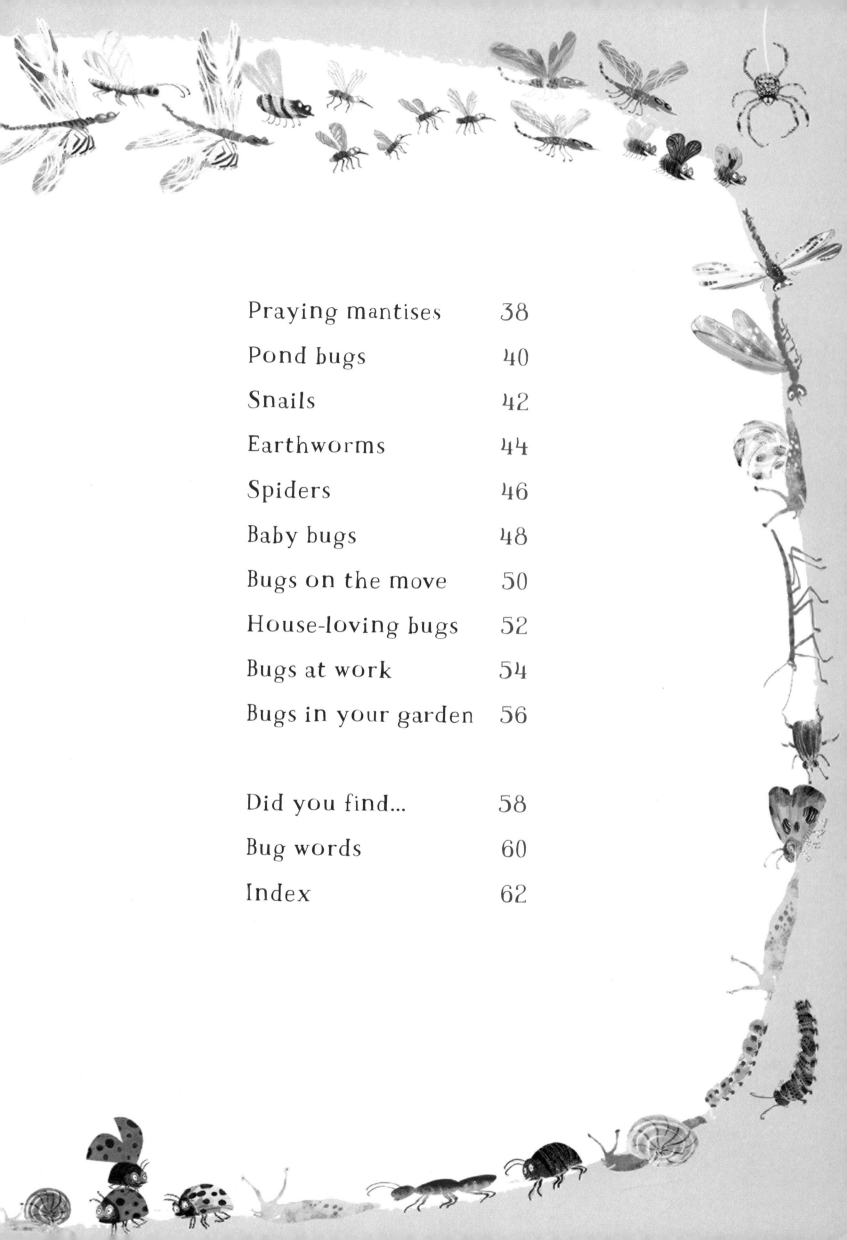

ALL KINDS OF BUGS

Who's inside this book?

Plenty of flying, stinging, wriggling bugs. Meet insects,
from buzzing bees to scuttling beetles, and all kinds of
creepy crawlies, such as snails, spiders, centipedes and worms.

What do they have in common?

They don't have bones inside their bodies.
Most bugs have a skeleton on the outside,
called an exoskeleton.

When is a bug not a bug?

Many people call all insects 'bugs', but to a scientist a bug is a particular kind of insect with sharp mouthparts to stab and suck up food.

Animals without backbones ...

... are called invertebrates. Insects are the biggest group of invertebrates.

BUG SPOTTERS

What does a bug think of you?

You are a giant to a teeny bug! In a bug's world, a flower is as tall as a tree and a rock is as high as a mountain. Let's go bug-spotting.

Bugs hide in dark places

They live under damp logs and stones and in dark flower pots.

Always be kind to bugs

Bugs don't like being picked up, but they don't mind being watched. Please look but don't touch.

BOOK OF BUGS

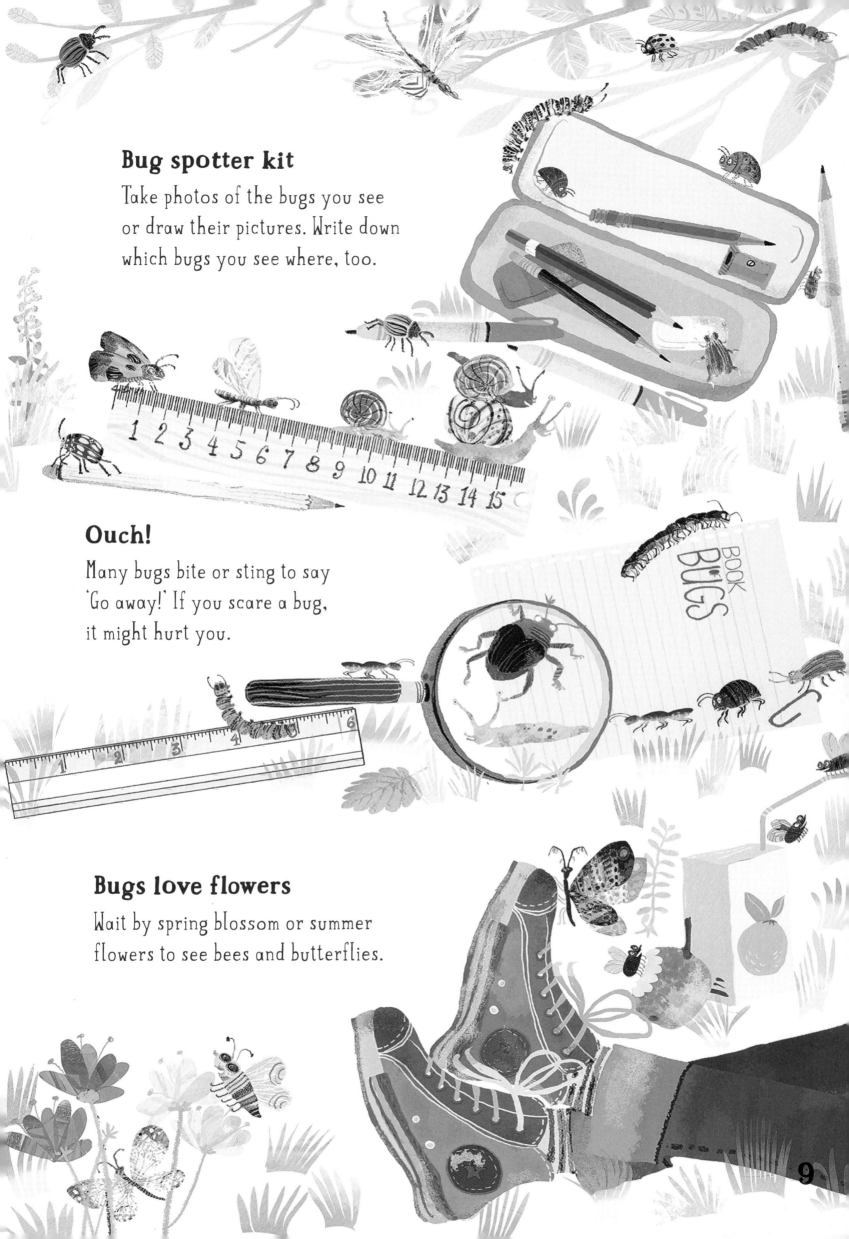

Bug spotter kit

Take photos of the bugs you see or draw their pictures. Write down which bugs you see where, too.

Ouch!

Many bugs bite or sting to say 'Go away!' If you scare a bug, it might hurt you.

Bugs love flowers

Wait by spring blossom or summer flowers to see bees and butterflies.

BUG FAMILY TREE

Are all bugs the same?

Not at all! Bugs come in different types, or families. Here's how to tell who's who.

Insects have ...

... a body in three parts
... six legs
... two, four or no wings
... feelers

Snails and slugs have ...

... one squishy 'foot' for sliding along
... feelers
... a shell that keeps a snail safe
... the scientific name 'gastropods'

Can you find ...

... two stick insects? Here's a clue - they look like thin twigs.

Spiders have ...

... eight legs

... no wings

... a body in two parts

... the scientific name 'arachnids'

Centipedes and millipedes have ...

... lots of legs

... a body made of a head plus many rings, or segments

... feelers

... the scientific name 'myriapods'

Worms have ...

... no legs

... a long bendy body

... a mouth at one end

... the scientific name 'annelids'

BEETLES

How does a beetle beetle along?

A beetle scuttles on six legs. It has a hard shell, like a suit of armour, to keep its wings safe.

Big beetle family

There are thousands of different kinds of beetles. They live in trees, water, sand, ice and even in your home.

Don't eat me!

Some beetles spray poison to say 'Leave me alone!'

Can you find ...

... two dung beetles rolling poo into big balls, ready to eat?

A baby beetle is wriggly

It hatches from an egg and is called a larva.

13

LADYBIRDS

How many spots are on a ladybird?

It depends because there are many different types.
A ladybird is a beetle and comes in all kinds of colours,
sizes and patterns. Some don't have spots at all.

Gardeners love ladybirds

Ladybirds eat small green bugs called
aphids. Aphids eat plants so a ladybird
is a gardener's best friend!

Ladybirds in space

Ladybirds have been taken up in a rocket to help with scientific research.

Warning! 'I'm poisonous!'

A ladybird's bright wings are a warning. They say 'I taste nasty'.

A ladybird sleeps all winter

It finds a dark place to hibernate with a group of other ladybirds.

15

BUTTERFLIES

How does a butterfly flutter by?

It flaps its beautiful wings and flies from flower to flower. It drinks a sweet juice, called nectar.

A butterfly has feelers to smell

It sucks up nectar through a long tube on its head.

A butterfly helps seeds to grow

It spreads a golden dust, called pollen, from flower to flower.

1

A butterfly changes

It starts as a tiny egg. A wriggly caterpillar hatches out and grows fat munching on leaves.

2

The caterpillar makes a shell ...

... called a chrysalis. Inside, it starts to change.

3

The shell splits open

The wriggling caterpillar has turned into a fluttering butterfly!

MOTHS

What does a moth do all day?

It hides. It's difficult to spot a moth against tree bark, leaves and even bird poo. At night, a moth flies around looking for sweet juices, such as flower nectar, to eat.

A moth's wings are dusty

Tiny hairs on its wings look and feel like dust. Never touch a moth's or a butterfly's wings, they might break!

Good at hiding

There are 29 moths in this picture. Can you find them all?

Some moths have 'pretend' eyes

The big spots on an owl moth's wings
look like eyes and scare enemies.

ANTS

Why do ants march in a line?

Because each ant follows the one in front. Thousands of ants share a nest. They work to keep the nest clean and safe and to bring back food.

An ant talks with its feelers

An ant taps its long feelers on other ants to pass on a message.

Ants follow smelly trails ...
... left by other ants to find food
to take back to the nest.

The queen lays many eggs
She is the mother of all the ants in
the nest. Most ants live for 90 days
but the queen ant can live for 15 years!

21

BEES

Why do bees buzz buzz buzz?

When a bee flaps its wings, it makes a buzzing noise. Honey bees buzz from flower to flower, helping more flowers to grow.

Honey bees live in a hive

Only the queen bee lays eggs. Worker bees do everything for the queen. They bring her food and help build, clean and guard the hive.

Can you find ...

... two stripey wasps among the bees? Look for thinner bodies. They also have biting jaws.

22

1

How do bees make honey?

A honey bee sucks up sweet nectar
from a flower with its long tongue. Then ...

2

... inside the hive ...

... the bees turn the nectar into
runny honey, ready for the
beekeeper to collect.

WILD FLOWER
HONEY

Dancing bees

Look back at the hive. Bees do a
waggle dance to tell each other
where to find fresh flowers.

NIGHT-TIME BUGS

Are bugs scared of the dark?

Not at all! Many bugs feel safer at night than during the day. In the dark, they can hide from bigger animals who want to eat them.

While butterflies sleep ...

... moths flutter around a honeysuckle plant because the flowers smell sweet in the evening air.

Flying towards the light

A bug finds its way by the light of the moon.
The bug can get confused by electric lights
and crash into them!

Can you find...

...a spider hoping to catch a tasty meal?

A glow worm's body shines

A glow worm says 'hello' to a mate
by flashing the light on its tail.

TERMITES

What do termites build?

Towers taller than a person, out of soil, spit, wood and poo. They also build round nests in trees. Some nests are underground.

Can you find ...

... a king termite and a queen termite flying away to build a new home?

Most termites are workers

Soldier termites guard the nest. Others collect plants and wood for food and look after the eggs.

Termites keep cool

Even though termites live in hot places, their towers are cool. Tall chimneys let hot air out of the nest.

FLIES

Why does a fly buzz around food?

It's hungry. It wants to eat the fresh food you like to eat. It also loves to suck up the sugary water in old, rotting food, which to a fly is full of goodness.

A fly is sick on its food

The sick softens up the food so the fly can slurp it up easily.

Can you find ...

... a caterpillar that has come to join the picnic?

28

A fly can walk upside down
A fly's feet ooze a sort of glue that helps it stick to things.

A fly is hard to catch
It flies fast, backwards, forwards and can even hover and spin.

A fly has special eyes
Each eye has more than 4000 lenses to help it pick up the slightest movement.

DRAGONFLIES

Does a dragonfly breathe fire?

No, a dragonfly is named after a dragon because it's a fierce hunter and good at flying. It can loop the loop and even fly backwards!

A dragonfly has huge eyes

A dragonfly spots insects from far away to zoom towards and eat.

Can you find ...

... a dragonfly that has
caught its dinner in mid-air?

Water babies

Baby dragonflies hatch from eggs
in water. They live in the water until,
one day, they grow wings and fly away.

CENTIPEDES

Does a centipede really have 100 legs?

Not always. Most centipedes have about 30 legs, but some have more than 300! A centipede marches along quickly on its legs. Up, two, three, four ...

A centipede has a bendy body

It has one pair of legs on each segment, or part, of its body.

Home is dark and damp

A centipede lives under leaves and logs. It needs to keep its body damp.

How big is a giant centipede?

As big as a dinner plate. A tropical giant
centipede eats frogs, birds and even bats.

Centipedes are very old

They lived on Earth long before dinosaurs appeared.

CRICKETS AND GRASSHOPPERS

Why do they chirp in the grass?

To find a partner. A male cricket or grasshopper chirps to get the attention of a female. Crickets and grasshoppers also chirp to say 'Look out! Danger!'

How do they make music?

A grasshopper rubs its back legs on its wings to chirp. A cricket rubs its wings together.

Can you find ...

... all the grasshoppers?
A grasshopper has short feelers, or antennae. A cricket has long ones.

34

They are good jumpers

A cricket and a grasshopper both have long back legs for jumping high.

They are bad flyers

Crickets and grasshoppers have two pairs of wings, but most aren't good at flying. And some can't fly at all.

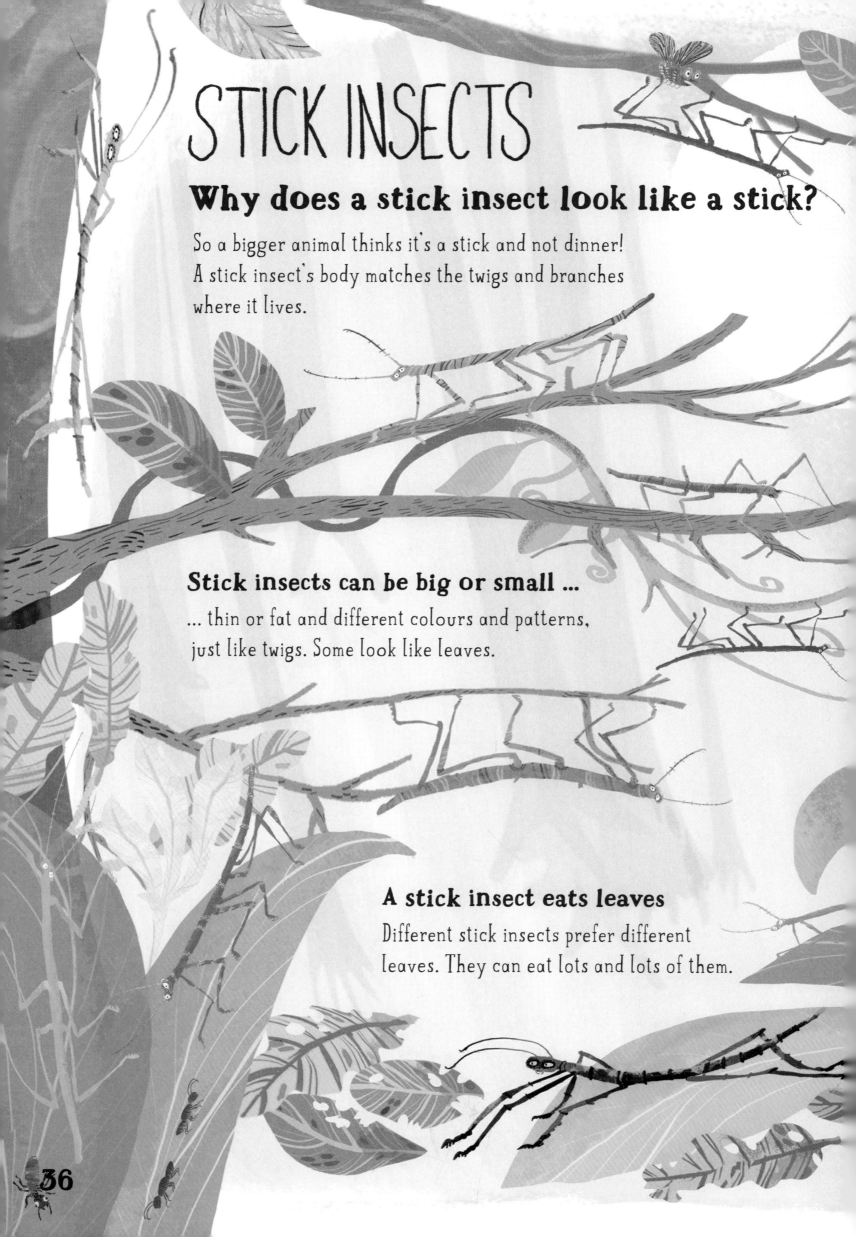

STICK INSECTS

Why does a stick insect look like a stick?

So a bigger animal thinks it's a stick and not dinner!
A stick insect's body matches the twigs and branches
where it lives.

Stick insects can be big or small ...

... thin or fat and different colours and patterns,
just like twigs. Some look like leaves.

A stick insect eats leaves

Different stick insects prefer different
leaves. They can eat lots and lots of them.

A stick insect can leave a leg behind

When a stick insect is trapped or in danger, it can break off a leg and run away. A new leg grows.

A female lays eggs

The babies hatch out and grow up alone.

Can you find ...

... two insects that look like leaves?

PRAYING MANTISES

Where does the name come from?

A mantis folds its long front legs together.
It looks like a person praying.

A praying mantis eats bugs alive

It grips the bug with its long, spiky
front legs. Then it eats the bug alive,
usually head first.

Can you find ...

... two praying mantises
eating dinner?

Can you find ...

...a praying mantis looking over its shoulder at you? It turns its bendy neck so its head faces backwards.

A female is bigger than a male

Often a female praying mantis eats a male! This gives her extra strength to lay lots of eggs.

POND BUGS

How does a bug walk on water?

With super-long legs. It slides and jumps over the top of the pond. It has a light body and it spreads its legs wide so it doesn't sink like we do.

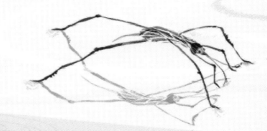

What happens underwater?

There are plenty of animals to eat. Bugs dart to catch food and scoot away from bigger animals that want to eat them.

Amazing snails

A pond snail can trap air in its shell to breathe under water. It can also breathe through its skin.

Can you find ...

... two backswimmer water beetles swimming upside down underwater? They have very strong legs.

A beetle with a snorkel

A water scorpion can float to the surface and take in air through a tube.

SNAILS

Just how slow does a snail go?

Super slow! It would take a snail about one day to slither to the end of a long garden.

A snail can see and sniff

A snail has four bendy feelers. Two long feelers have eyes on the tips. Two shorter feelers sniff things to eat.

A shell is a safe home

But watch out! A bird might smash the shell and eat the snail inside.

Snails live in wet places

They leave a slimy trail, which helps them to glide along.

A snail lays eggs

Baby snails hatch out. As the snail grows, its shell grows too.

43

EARTHWORMS

Why do earthworms wriggle?

They don't have legs so they stretch and slither to move along. They grip the ground with tiny hairs all over their bodies.

Good for the garden

An earthworm digs tunnels and lets air into the soil. This helps plants to grow.

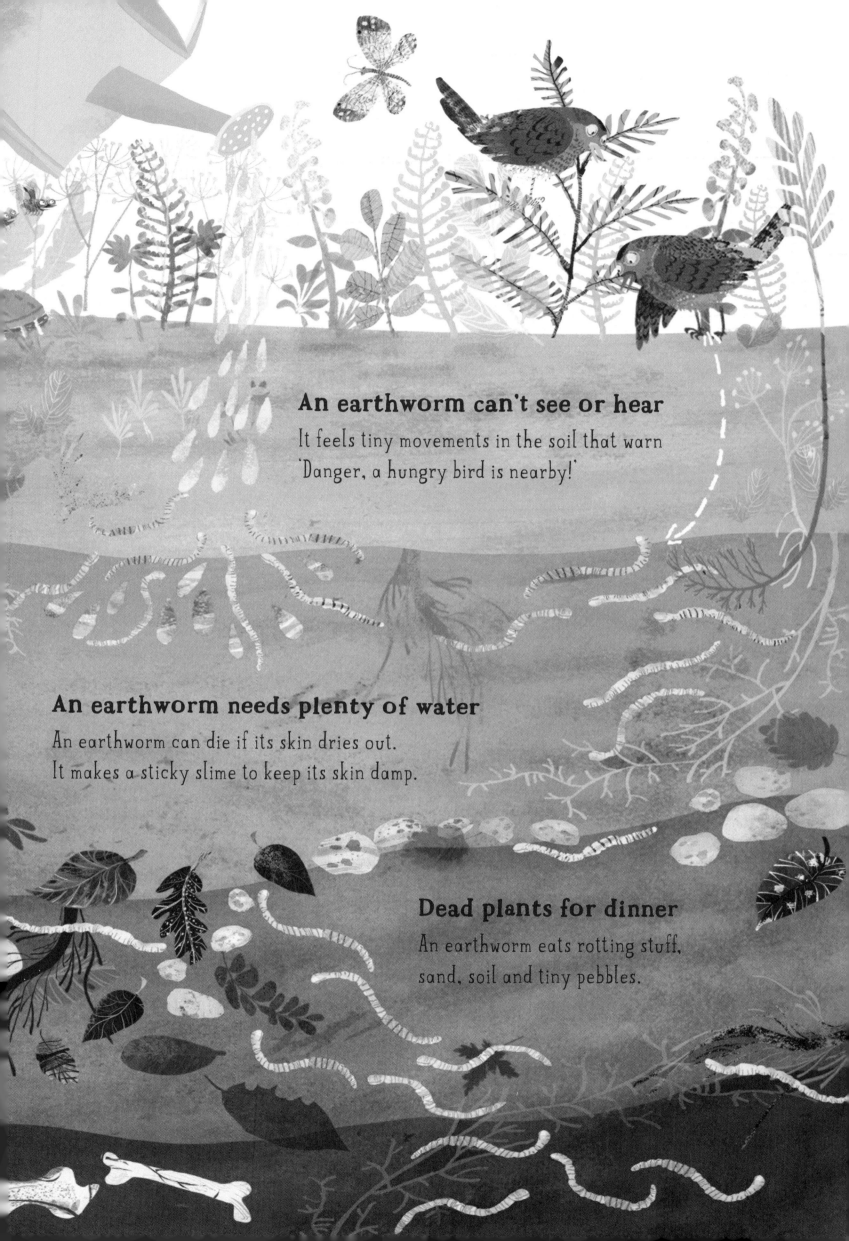

An earthworm can't see or hear

It feels tiny movements in the soil that warn
'Danger, a hungry bird is nearby!'

An earthworm needs plenty of water

An earthworm can die if its skin dries out.
It makes a sticky slime to keep its skin damp.

Dead plants for dinner

An earthworm eats rotting stuff,
sand, soil and tiny pebbles.

SPIDERS

How many legs does a spider have?

A spider has eight hairy legs and 48 knees.
Some spiders have long legs, others have short
fat legs. There are many different kinds of spider.

A spider is really hairy

It uses its hairs to taste, hear and touch.
The hairs pick up tiny movements.

A spider has eight eyes ...

... but it can't see things well
if they are far away.

46

**A spider pulls silk
out of its body**

It spins a web with long, strong
strands of silk and catches
flying bugs for dinner.

Can you find ...

... a trapdoor spider that builds
a trap to catch dinner?

BABY BUGS

Does a baby bug look like its parents?

A baby snail looks like a tiny snail but a baby beetle starts off as a squirmy grub called a larva. Look at the changes it goes through to become a beetle.

adult

larva

egg

Most bugs hatch from eggs

How many eggs can you count in this picture? Which bugs do they belong to?

Most bugs don't look after their eggs

But a female spider does. She gently carries a sack of eggs in her jaws.

Fly off to page 16 to find out how a caterpillar changes into a butterfly.

Can you find ...

... the old crumpled skin of a centipede? As a centipede grows, it sheds its old skin and a new one grows.

A dung beetle lays eggs in poo ...

... to make sure that its babies have food when they hatch.

HOUSE-LOVING BUGS
Why do bugs like to be indoors?

The same reasons as you. It is warm, dry and full of tasty food. A bug has an easy life inside your house.

A spider is a wonderful house guest

It sits quietly in its web, catching and eating flies that want to steal your food.

Can you find ...

... a family of silverfish? A silverfish is a tiny grey insect with three prongs on its tail.

A cockroach eats anything

A cockroach scuttles around at night eating anything it can find, including glue, paper, soap and shoe polish.

A dust mite sucks up dead skin

Millions of teeny dust mites live in your house. They eat the tiny flakes of dead skin that make up dust.

WELCOME

CEREAL

BUGS IN YOUR GARDEN

How can you make bugs welcome?

Whether you've got a big garden, a small garden or just a windowsill, you can help bugs by giving them food and a place to live.

BUTTERFLY BREAKFAST

Butterfly breakfast

Plant flower seeds in your garden or window boxes. Watch butterflies and insects drink flower nectar for breakfast.

CATERPILLAR CAFÉ

Caterpillar café

An egg box is the perfect place for hungry caterpillars to feast. Fill it with juicy green leaves and soft grass.

BEE HOTEL

Make a bee hotel

Tie together a few stems of bamboo. Push them to fit snugly into a flower pot. Use string to hang the pot from a shaded, low tree branch.

CREEPY CRAWLY CAMPSITE

Creepy crawly campsite

Fill a container with dead and rotting wood, leaves and moss for bugs to eat and explore.

57

BUG WORDS

How to talk like a bug expert

Here are some words to use when you talk about bugs.

Bug bodies

An insect's body is in three main parts. The head, **thorax** and **abdomen**.

A bug smells and feels with feelers called **antennae**.

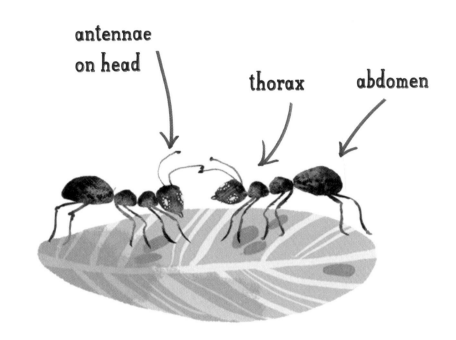

antennae on head

thorax

abdomen

An insect is an **invertebrate**, which means it doesn't have a backbone. Instead, insects have a hard **exoskeleton** outside their bodies.

Staying alive

Bugs avoid other hungry animals, or **predators**. Some bugs stay safe by blending in with the background. This is called **camouflage**.

Some bugs use warning colours to show that they are **poisonous**, or dangerous to eat.

Feeding from flowers

A bug visits plants to drink **nectar**, which is a delicious sweet juice.

Pollen is a golden sticky dust found on flowers. Many bugs carry pollen from one plant to another and help new seeds to grow.

A bug's life ...

... is called a **life cycle**. Many bugs start life as an **egg**, which hatches into a squirmy grub called a **larva**, which then grows into an **adult**.

In the life cycle of a butterfly, the **larva** is called a caterpillar. The caterpillar makes a hard shell called a **chrysalis**, or **pupa**. Inside it changes into a butterfly.

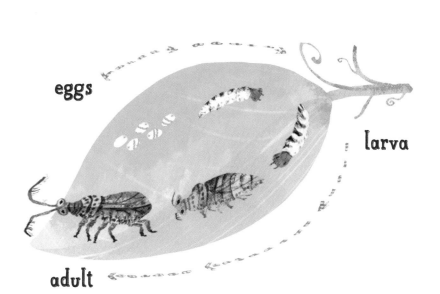

eggs

larva

adult

To my big sister Navit, with all my love.

First published in the United Kingdom in 2016 by
Thames & Hudson Ltd,
181A High Holborn,
London WC1V 7QX

The Big Book of Bugs © 2016 Yuval Zommer

British Library Cataloguing-in-Publication Data
A catalogue record for this book is available from
the British Library

ISBN 978-0-500-65067-7

Printed and bound in Slovenia by DZS-Grafik d.o.o.

To find out about all our publications, please visit
www.thamesandhudson.com. There you can subscribe
to our e-newsletter, browse or download our current
catalogue, and buy any titles that are in print.